DRY BONES...
and other fossils

Gary E. Parker, M.S., Ed.D.

Illustrated by

Jonathan Chong

Read-along
Cassette
NEW! for children
(70 minutes)
Available

M3 Master Books

Dry Bones . . . and Other Fossils
Copyright ©1979

First printing 1979
Second printing 1980
Third printing 1983
Fourth printing 1985
Revised Edition 1987

 Dry Bones Read-along Cassette (70 minutes)
New Entertaining and Educational ©1986

Production: Creantis Vox

Story Character Played by
"Dr Parker" . . . . . . Dr. Gary Parker
"David" . . . . Joel Murphy
"Diane" . . . . Genevieve Unfred
"Dana" . . . . Deedra Lindsey
"Debbie" . . . . Janelle Tepfer

Original Music — Jeff and Gail Bones

Printed in the United States of America

Creation-Life Publishers, Inc.
Master Books Division
P.O. Box 1606
El Cajon, California 92022

Library of Congress Catalog Card Number 79-51174
ISBN 0-89051-056-3

Cataloging in Publication Data
Parker, Gary E. 1940 -
   Dry bones . . . and other fossils
    1. Paleontology — Juvenile literature. I. Chong, Jonathan, 1956 -   , ill.
II. Title.
                      560   79-51174
ISBN 0-89051-056-3

CONTENTS

INTRODUCTION

Did you ever dream that you were hunting dinosaurs? Or that you found a lost valley full of all kinds of strange creatures, such as flying lizards and giant beavers?

Well, you can do it for real! Dinosaurs and giant sea scorpions and all kinds of creatures from the past are still out there just waiting to be found — as fossils! Fossils are parts of plants and animals preserved in rock. All you need

Fossils

to find them is a sharp eye, a small pick hammer, a sack, and a little background information.

To give you a little more background, I would like to use this book to take you fossil hunting with my family and me. I am Dr. Gary Parker, a scientist with training in fossil study (paleontology — pay lee on 'tol o gee). My wife's name is Mary and our four children are Dana, Debbie, David, and Diane.

We have found over half a ton of fossils from all over North America, and we would like to share our adventures and our thoughts about fossils with you.

So, crank up your imagination, and we will take you on a fossil hunting trip with us! Ready? We have just stepped out of the car where the road cuts through a a hill in southern Indiana . . .

Chapter One

What Are Fossils? How Are They Formed?

Hey, Dad, what is this?

What does it look like, Dave?

It looks like a snail.

That's what it is.

Why is it so hard just like a rock?

Actually, Dave, it's a fossil.

A fossil?

What is a fossil?

A fossil is a plant or animal preserved in rock. A very few were trapped in ice or tar, but most were trapped in lime, mud, or sand that turned into rock.

How did it get trapped, Dad?

Probably a flood did it. That's how most fossils were started.

What about this snail in my hand, Dad?

It was probably crawling around, just minding its own business. Then all of a sudden, "whoosh," mud from a river flood or from a big underwater landslide swept up the snail. So, it was buried with all the other snails and clams you see around here.

Why didn't the snail just crawl out of the mud?

Good point, Dave. That's why it takes a big flood to start forming fossils. Mud or sand just settling out of a lake or ocean would never stop a snail; that's for sure.

What if the snail were already dead?

If the snail died and just fell to the bottom, the waves would break it apart, or it would rot or be eaten by other animals. The buffaloes shot by the cowboys and Indians never turned into fossils. The parts that were left just rotted away on top of the ground.

I get it, Dad. It takes something like a flood to start forming a fossil. The animal gets buried too deeply to crawl out, and the heavy layer

of sand or mud keeps the waves or other animals from tearing it up.

Right, Dave.

But what made the fossil snail become hard like a rock?

You have watched people mix concrete, haven't you?

Sure.

What happens?

It starts off slushy when you mix the sand and cement and water. Then it dries out and turns hard.

Almost. Actually, the concrete cures, instead of drying out. The water helps the cement minerals stick together, and they lock up the sand particles to form a hard, man-made rock.

Okay, Dad. I know about concrete. But why is this fossil snail so hard?

First, the snail was trapped in the mud. Next the minerals in the mud started to stick together, as they do in concrete, and the mud turned into rock. Then, in this case, the snail shell dissolved away as the extra water was squeezed out. What is left is that rock in your hand, which is formed in the shape of a snail.

 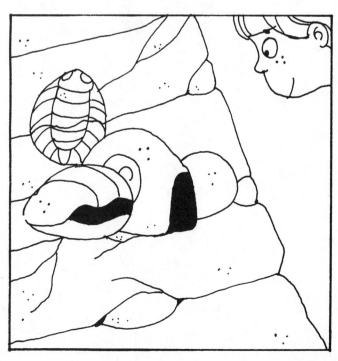

Is this a petrified snail?

Almost, but not quite. In a petrified fossil, the rock minerals fill in the exact place of some part of the plant or animal. In petrified wood, the minerals fill in all the spaces as the mud turns into rock. Look at all the details in this piece of petrified wood I have here in my pocket.

Wow! You can even see the rings!

You can see a lot of your snail, too. You can see the spines and twists and the hole where the animal came out. But none of the snail is really there. You have just a mold.

A mold?

What is a mold?

A mold is made when you push your finger into a lump of clay and see the outline. Here the mud was pushed up into your snail shell, and now you can see the outline of what the snail looked like on the inside. See this rock here?

Oh, yes. It's just a dent in the rock, but it still looks like a snail.

Right. This is an "outside mold" of the snail. When the mud hardened around the old snail shell, it took on the shape of the snail. Then the old shell dissolved away. If that hole had filled in with some other mineral, then we would have a "cast" showing the shape of the snail. Molds and casts and petrified things are all different kinds of fossils.

Here is another kind of fossil I like to keep in my pocket, Dave. What does that look like?

It looks to me like stuff that dogs drop on the yard, Dad.

You are almost right. Instead of dog dung, though, it's a fossil dinosaur dropping.

Ugh! Take it back!

Don't worry. It's a special fossil called a "coprolite" **('cō pro lite)**. It doesn't smell, and it can't come off on your hand. It has already turned into rock.

How about that. So a fossil starts when living things get trapped in mud or sand from a flood. Then when the rock hardens, the plants and animals that were trapped turn into fossils. Right?

That's right, Dave.

Here's another fossil, Dad. What kind is it?

That's a piece of coral.

Coral? I thought corals only lived in the ocean.

That's right. But all these other things lived in the ocean, too. That snail you had is an ocean snail. This is an ocean clam, and this is an ocean lamp shell. Over there is a piece of squid shell from the ocean. This is part of an ocean animal in the starfish group.

*How did all these **ocean** animals get to **Indiana?***

Well, most fossils start out as plants and animals trapped in sediment (**'sed ĭ ment**). Sediment is the mud or sand that settles from flood waters. Do you know of any flood big enough to wash ocean life all the way to Indiana?

Noah's Flood?

Sure, why not? The Bible tells us that the Flood covered the whole earth. Stories from tribes all over the world also tell about the Flood.

Did the Flood really cover the whole earth?

It surely looks like it. Flood sediment covers over three-fourths of all the land on earth. You can even find fossils of ocean life on top of high mountains. First, all the land was covered. Then, the Bible tells us, the mountains rose up and the valleys sank down at the end of the Flood.

Did Noah's Flood make all the fossils?

The Bible doesn't tell us for sure. But the Flood would surely help us explain much of what we see. After all, fossils start as plants and animals which have been trapped in flood sediment. Then as the land rises and dries out after the Flood, all the mud and sand would begin turning into rock. And the plants and animals trapped in the sediment would turn into fossils.

Are any fossils forming today?

Any time a plant or animal gets buried under enough mud or sand, it could start becoming a fossil — **if** the mud or sand had the right minerals and conditions to turn into rock. But the rock layers with fossils we are standing on cover a big part of Indiana, Ohio, and Kentucky. There is no place in the world today where fossils are forming that way! This would take something like Noah's Flood for sure!

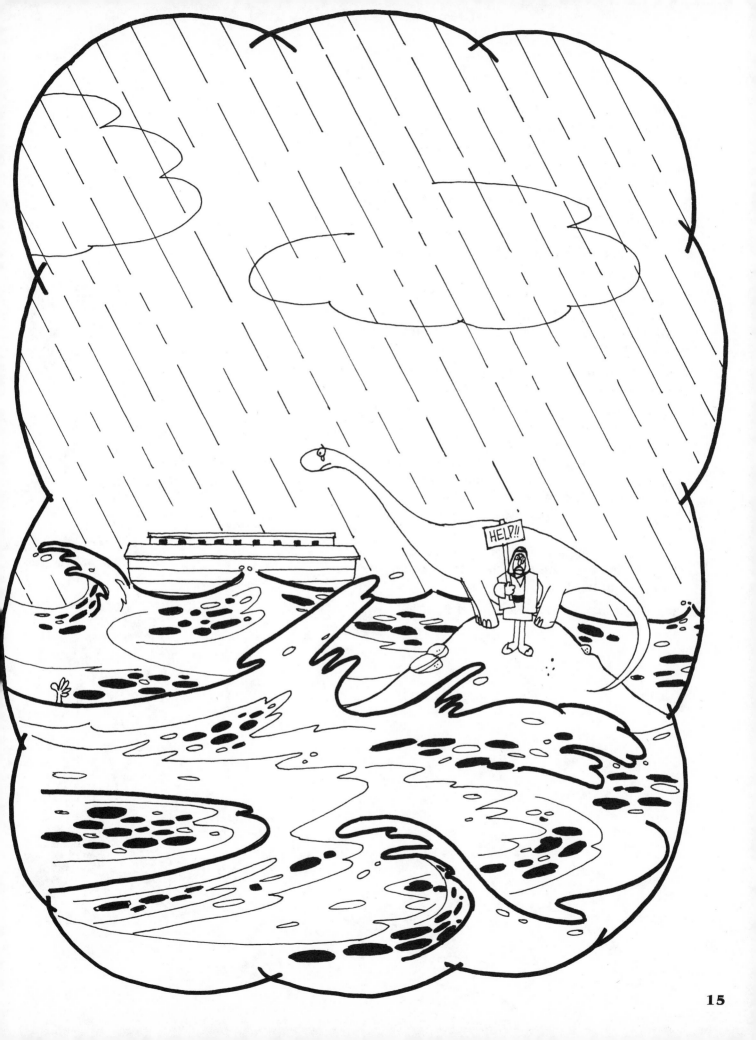

Why did God send the Flood that killed all those plants and animals?

That's one of the saddest stories in the Bible. It started with the sin of our first parents, Adam and Eve. Because of their sin, the whole world was cursed, and soon the earth was filled with violence. All this violence and wickedness grieved God's heart. The Bible even says He was sorry He made the world.

What did God do?

God sent the great Flood to destroy evil and give the world a fresh start with Noah and his family, as well as the animals they took on the Ark.

Are the fossils all the plants, animals, and people that were drowned in the Flood?

That's probably right, Dave. And you know what? If that's so, then you and I are standing right here on a huge graveyard. And all these fossils that cover the world tell us about the evil effect of violence and sin, and they remind us of God's judgment.

Will God ever destroy the world again?

Well, the earth is full of violence and sin again, isn't it? The Apostle Peter tells us this world will be destroyed by fire.

What will happen to everybody then?

That depends. The people who hate God will go on hating Him forever, unless they turn to Him for forgiveness. God has something very special for the people who are sorry for their sins and turn to Him.

What's that, Dad?

A new heaven and new earth, where God lives with His people, and there is no more sin and violence. So, think of that the next time we go fossil hunting, Dave.

What do you mean?

All the fossils buried in the earth remind us how God hates sin and how powerful His judgment is.

But if God can keep His promise to punish sin, then God will keep His promise of new heavens and a new earth for people who love Him. Right?

Right, Dave.

Chapter 2

What Kinds of Living Things Are Found as Fossils?

Was it easy to imagine yourself hunting fossils by the roadside with David and me? I hope so. I hope David's questions helped you to start thinking about fossils, too — *what* fossils are, *how* they are formed, and *where* fossils fit into Bible history.

But I imagine you still have many more questions. So did my youngest daughter, Diane. As soon as we got home, she started asking questions about the fossils we found. Before long, I had to take her down to the Museum. We looked at the different kinds of fossil plants and animals there.

Do you want to come along? We'll stop by the house first and pick up Diane.

Say, Dad, is this the fossil snail that David found when you went fossil hunting?

It surely is.

David said this snail was drowned and buried in Noah's Flood. Is that right?

It seems to be. That's probably why we find fossils of sea life all over the earth. The Flood covered the whole earth.

You mean this snail was probably alive when Noah was alive? Wow! What other kinds of plants and animals lived on the earth back in those days?

Want to go down to the Museum and see?

Sure!

(You can come, too, when you visit San Diego. Until then, get your imagination working again. Let's walk through the doors into the Museum of Creation and Earth History at the Institute for Creation Research.)

Over here, Diane, is the display case that shows some of the first kinds of ocean creatures we find as fossils. Do you see any you can recognize?

Yes, lots of them. There is a fish. There is a snail like we find at the beach.

Anything else?

Well, there is a razor clam, and a mussel, and, I think you call this one a scallop. That one looks like a starfish and this one is a piece of coral. Dad, are you sure these are fossils? They look like the shells we found at the beach last Saturday.

They **are** fossils. But you are right, Diane. They **do** look like fish and seashells today.

Why do fossil shells look so much like shells today, Dad?

Can you answer that? Just think a minute.

Hmm. Well, let's see. God created all the animals. So I guess if God created snails and clams, then fossil snails and clams should just look like snails and clams.

Good thinking, Diane. Now take a look over here. This mural shows the fossils of plants we find. What do you see?

There is an oak tree, a willow tree, and a palm. Over here is a magnolia and a pine, and there are lots of ferns. Do you mean fossil plants are just ordinary plants?

Most of them are. Over here are some of the bony animals that were buried in the Flood. Like today, there are different kinds of fish and birds and turtles and bats and antelopes. So, from the fossils, it looks like snails have always been snails, oak trees always oak trees, and birds always birds.

You mean the fossil plants and animals living way back at the beginning before the Flood are like plants and animals today?

21

They are similar. Most of the things we find as fossils are like plants and animals living today. But some are different. What is that fossil on the shelf in front of you?

Ugh! I don't know. It looks like a pill bug, except it has great big eyes.

That's a trilobite.

A what-o-bite?

A trilobite (**'try lō bīte**). It does look like a pill bug. It has a tough shell and lots of legs. But it also has big compound eyes like a grasshopper.

Neat! But why haven't I ever seen one? Where do they live, Dad?

They once lived in the ocean. But no more, Diane. They are extinct (**ex 'tinkt**).

Extinct? What does that mean?

That means they died out. Judging from the fossils, the world once had many trilobites crawling around on the ocean floor. But no more. They all died off, or became extinct.

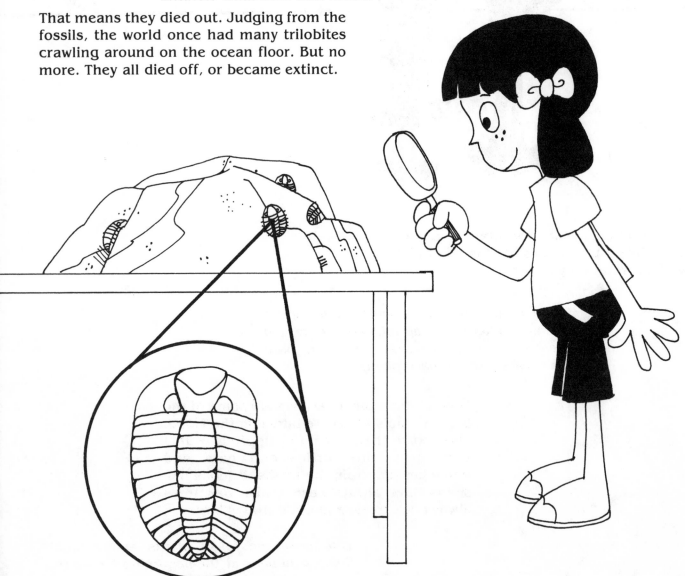

Why did they die and become extinct, Dad?

They probably died in the great Flood. A lot of water creatures probably survived the Flood easily. But trilobites lived on the bottom and couldn't swim too well, so maybe they were all buried. Many other animals probably also died in the Flood or shortly afterward. Remember when we went to the La Brea Tar Pits in Los Angeles, Diane?

Yes. We saw big, hairy elephants stuck in the tar, and a tiger with great big teeth.

There was an Indian woman, too. Those elephants and sabertoothed tigers lived in Los Angeles not too long ago, but they died out.

Why?

Maybe they couldn't live in the different climate after the Flood, or maybe people hunted them to extinction.

23

Here is a picture of another extinct creature, Diane. Do you know what it is?

Of course! It's a dinosaur! Did dinosaurs live when Noah lived, Dad?

That's what I think. After all the Bible tells us that God created all the animals the same day He created people. The way it looks, dinosaurs were drowned in the Flood too.

Oh yes! I guess if man and dinosaur had lived together, they could have made footprints at the same time, too.

That's right. But if their footprints were made together, who do you suppose was chasing whom, Diane?

I bet the dinosaur was chasing the man!

Maybe not. After all, people used to hunt giant mammoth elephants with spears, and men with harpoons nearly hunted certain whales to extinction. Did you know the biggest whale is over twice as big by weight as the biggest dinosaur?

Really? I didn't know that.

*The evidence for man and dinosaurs living at the same time before and after the Flood is presented in the exciting, new, full-color book by Paul Taylor, *The Great Dinosaur Mystery and the Bible*, published by Master Books, P.O. Box 1606, El Cajon, CA 92022.

By the way, Dad, if dinosaurs were alive when the Flood came, did Noah have to take them on the Ark?

He surely did. God told Noah to take at least one pair of all the dry land animals.

How did they all fit on the Ark?

No problem, believe it or not. Of course, Noah probably took young adults. But the Ark was so big, it could hold over 500 railroad boxcars full of animals with space left over!

Well, if the dinosaurs were on the Ark, why don't we see them today?

It could be the climate. Before the Flood, it was warm and mild and lush green over the whole earth. Did you know there are fossils of alligators and tropical plants in Greenland and Alaska?

Really? How did that happen, Dad?

Well, before the Flood it seems that there was extra water vapor in the air and more of that stuff called carbon dioxide. That would make the plants grow better and keep the earth warm, like a greenhouse.

So I guess the dinosaurs would have more to eat, and they could grow all year long. Maybe that's why they got so big.

You might be right, Diane. Did you know that there are many other giant fossils that have been found?

Really? What were they?

There was a giant sea scorpion over seven feet long, and a dragonfly over two feet across! There were even giant beavers six feet long! Maybe they used to cut down the giant trees that look like the little horsetails and club mosses we have today!

Wow! Is that what the Bible means about "giants in the earth in those days?"

Maybe. There were also giant races of men on earth in those days, too. Only a few are that big today.

What happened to all those giant plants and animals?

A lot of them probably drowned in the Flood. Some of them were in the Ark with Noah. But, like the dinosaurs, maybe they couldn't find enough food or the right climate after the Flood.

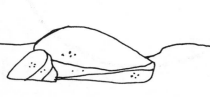

Why did things change after the Flood, Dad?

> It seems that much of the water vapor blanket around the earth fell as rain during the Flood, so the earth isn't as warm today. And much of the carbon dioxide got tied up in the limestone rock that formed in the Flood. That affected plant growth and climate, too.

Are there more deserts and snow and ice today than when Noah was alive?

> It surely seems that way, Diane. And before the Flood, there were many more plants without seeds, compared to seed plants. Plants without seeds didn't survive the Flood as well as seed plants. So maybe some animals died out because the plants they ate died out.

That makes me wish Adam and Eve had never sinned.

> Why do you say that, Diane?

Then God wouldn't have had to send the Flood, and there would be many more plants and animals on earth. It might have taken three days to see all the animals in the whole zoo back when Noah was alive.

> I think you're right, Diane.

Say, Dad, I was just thinking.

What?

Well, the fossils are good news and bad news.

What do you mean, Diane?

The good news is that fossils show how wonderful God is to create all the different kinds of life.

What's the bad news?

A lot of plants and animals became extinct because our sins made the world so bad that God had to send the Flood.

But there's still good news at the end, Diane.

What's that?

God told Isaiah that when Christ comes, "the wolf shall dwell with the lamb . . . and they shall not hurt or destroy in all my holy mountain, but the earth shall be full of the knowledge of the Lord, as the waters cover the sea."

I'll like that, Dad.

I will too, Diane! It is something we should always keep in our prayers.

Chapter 3

Why Are Fossils Found in Groups?

Did you enjoy the trip to the Museum with Diane and me? I hope you noticed that most fossils are ordinary kinds of life. They are just snails, clams, fish, fern leaves, and so on. That makes fossil collecting easier, since most things you find look like plants and animals living today.

But a lot of things have died out, or become extinct. That could be because of the Flood and the change in climate afterward. Many giant things became extinct, like six-foot beavers, two-foot dragonflies, and those "terrible lizards," the dinosaurs.*

And that reminds me. I promised to take you on a dinosaur hunt.

Here comes my oldest daughter, Dana, with a big bucket full of fossils. Maybe she found some dinosaur bones, and can tell us where to look. (I wasn't having much luck, as you can see!)

*"Dino-saur" means "terrible lizard." Learn more about dinosaurs in a full color children's book by Dr. Duane Gish, *Dinosaurs: Those Terrible Lizards* (Master Books, P.O. Box 1606, El Cajon, CA 92022).

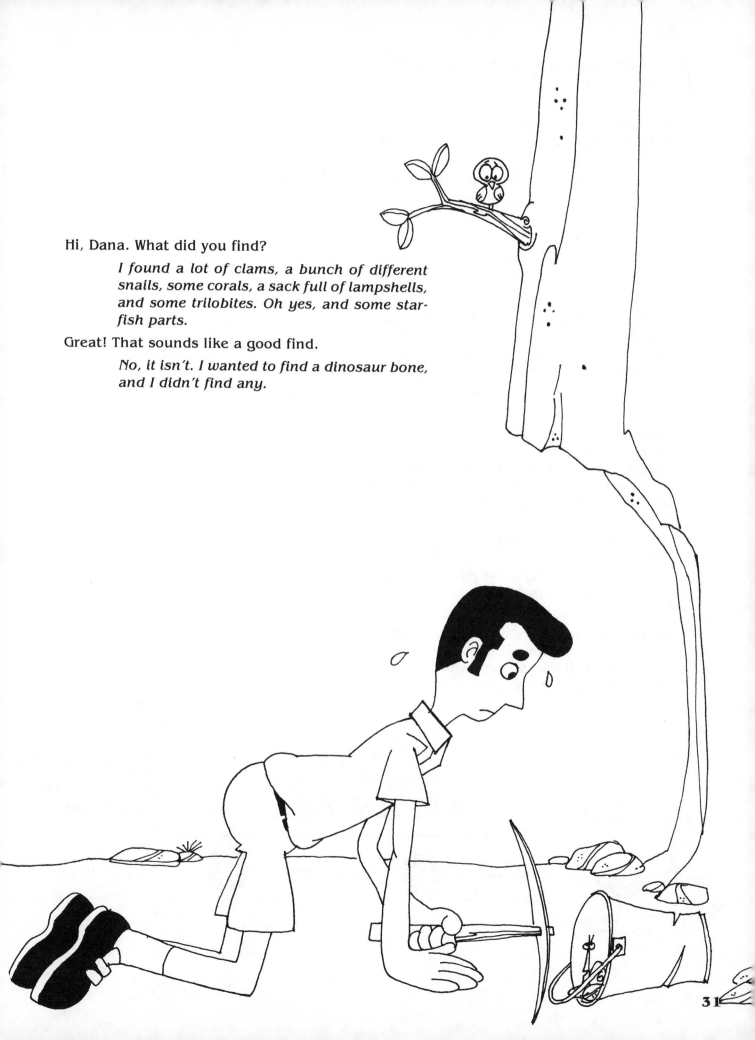

Hi, Dana. What did you find?

I found a lot of clams, a bunch of different snails, some corals, a sack full of lampshells, and some trilobites. Oh yes, and some starfish parts.

Great! That sounds like a good find.

No, it isn't. I wanted to find a dinosaur bone, and I didn't find any.

31

You didn't expect to find any dinosaur bones here, did you, Dana?

Sure, why not?

Think a minute. Look at all those fossils you found — snails, clams, corals, and starfish. Those are all sea creatures.

Oh, I get it. Dinosaurs lived on the land. I guess you wouldn't find them with sea creatures, would you?

That's right, Dana.

Well, where can we go to find some dinosaur bones, Dad?

There is a great place along the northern boundary of Utah and Colorado, and a new area below San Diego in Mexico. And this summer we are going to hunt dinosaur bones in Alberta, Canada, near Drumheller.

Why do you find dinosaurs in all those places?

That's probably just where they got buried. As you know, plants and animals live in groups. Squirrels live in the forest; alligators live in swamps; and certain kinds of lizards live in the desert. So as the Flood waters began to rise over the earth, it buried fossils in certain groups according to where they lived.

Hmm. So those places you named, Dad, are where the dinosaurs lived before the Flood. Is that right?

Almost. The dinosaurs probably got carried by the Flood waters quite a distance first. But at least those places would be near where they used to live.

Red Deer River Valley 2½ mi

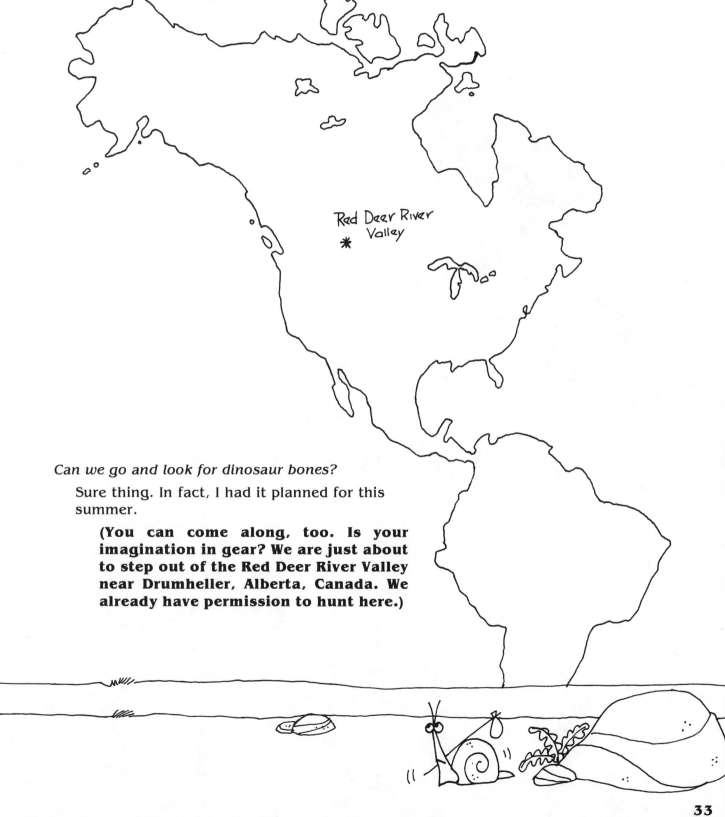

Red Deer River Valley

*

Can we go and look for dinosaur bones?

Sure thing. In fact, I had it planned for this summer.

(You can come along, too. Is your imagination in gear? We are just about to step out of the Red Deer River Valley near Drumheller, Alberta, Canada. We already have permission to hunt here.)

Wow, Dad! Look at all these bones! I wish I could find a whole one! Can you tell what these pieces are?

Most of the pieces are really too small to tell for sure, Dana. But I think I can identify some. That looks like a piece of rib, and that big chunk is probably part of the backbone.

Come over here and help me dig out this
dinosaur foot bone, Dana! Careful! We'll
need to wrap it in plastered gauze.

Great hunting, Dad!

We did get some nice specimens, but
nothing good enough to report to the
museum in Drumheller.

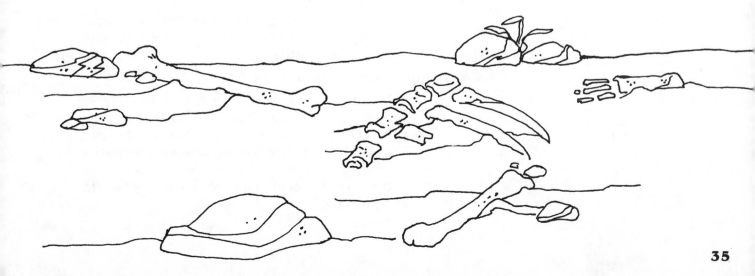

By the way, Dana, did you find any corals or starfish?

No, I didn't. I didn't find any lampshells or trilobites like we found in Indiana and Iowa, either.

Why not?

I suppose because dinosaurs and sea creatures didn't live together before the Flood. So, naturally, you wouldn't expect to find them buried in the same place.

I think you're right, Dana. So in a way, each group of fossils is an ecological zone **(e ko̅ 'loj i kul)**.

An ecological zone — what's that?

It's like a forest, a swamp, a desert, a lake, a prairie, or a rocky beach. An ecological zone is just an area where certain plants and animals live. The fossils probably show us what plants and animals lived together in the various ecological zones in the world before the Flood.

*So these bones we found here would be in the
dinosaur zone, and the corals and snails and
lampshells we found in Indiana and Iowa
would be an ocean zone.*

Right. Scientists even have special names
for different fossil zones or groups. These
dinosaur bones belong to the Cretaceous
group. That's **"Kree 'tay shus."**

*Are there other groups of fossils with big
names like that, Dad?*

Yes, Dana, about a dozen main groups in all.
A group of fossils that is mostly trilobites
and lampshells is called the Cambrian
(**'Kam brē un**) for example, and the group
named after the state of Pennsylvania has a
lot of coal in it.

Dad, how was the coal formed?

Coal probably started out as a lush lowland forest, with lots of tree ferns and other fern-like plants.

Do we still have plants like that today?

Most of them died out, but we still have quite a few, mostly in tropical areas.

What happened to the old coal forest plants?

Well, Dana, as the Flood waters started to rise, the sediments first began to bury a lot of the ocean bottom creatures. Then as the Flood waters rose higher and the currents became stronger, they started to rip out the coal forest trees and sweep them away.

Was it like a tropical storm, where groups of trees wash off in great big mats?

Yes, much like that. Some mats of vegetation have washed from the Amazon River 600 miles out to sea. In some mats after storms in the Pacific you can even see palm trees floating upright.

You mean the palm trees can be standing straight up and down? How do they do that, Dad? Wouldn't they lie flat?

Try this experiment, Dana. **(You can try it, too.)** Next time you are sipping a soda through a straw, put a piece of gum on the end of the straw and toss it into the glass. I think it will float upright. And that's the way with a lot of hollow-stemmed trees; they stand upright through several layers of coal.

So, coal started as a group of trees ripped up and washed along in a mat by the Flood.

That's right, Dana. And there are many other things that make coal look like a Flood deposit, too. The solid logs show the direction of current flow, for instance, and some ocean worms attached to the coal plants while they floated.

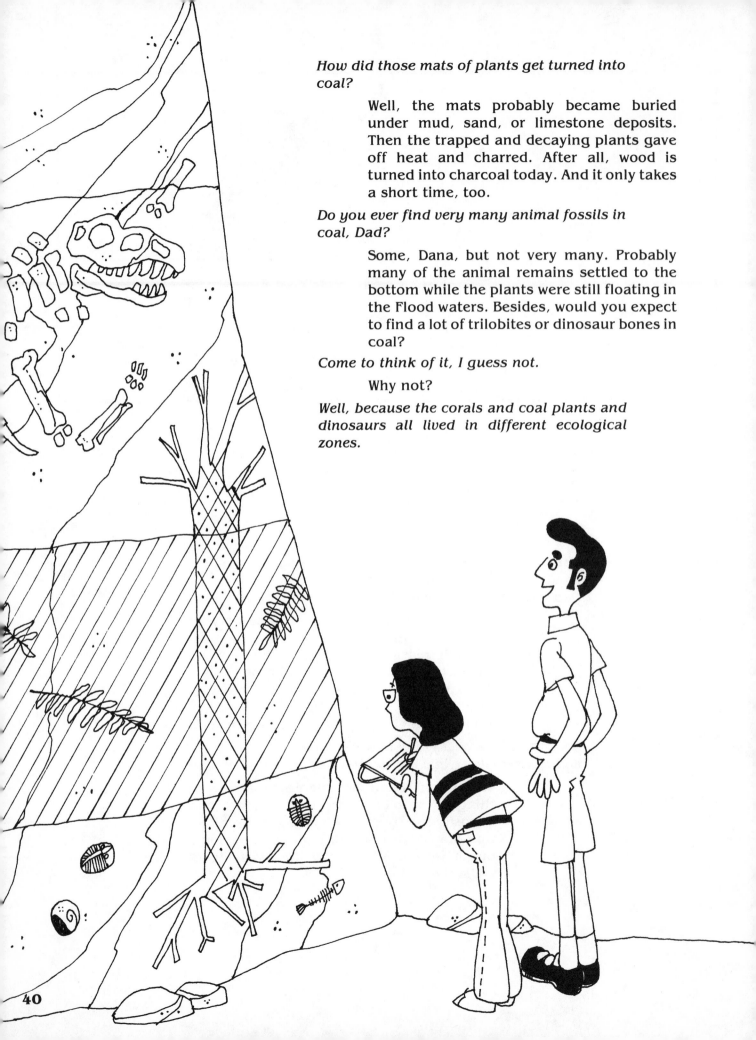

How did those mats of plants get turned into coal?

Well, the mats probably became buried under mud, sand, or limestone deposits. Then the trapped and decaying plants gave off heat and charred. After all, wood is turned into charcoal today. And it only takes a short time, too.

Do you ever find very many animal fossils in coal, Dad?

Some, Dana, but not very many. Probably many of the animal remains settled to the bottom while the plants were still floating in the Flood waters. Besides, would you expect to find a lot of trilobites or dinosaur bones in coal?

Come to think of it, I guess not.

Why not?

Well, because the corals and coal plants and dinosaurs all lived in different ecological zones.

That's using your head! But suppose you found two fossil rock layers, one on top of the other. What would you expect on the bottom: the trilobites, or the coal, or the dinosaurs?

Probably the trilobites.

Why do you say that, Dana?

Well, the trilobites are ocean bottom creatures, so they were probably buried first in the Flood. The plants and dinosaurs that lived on land were washed in on top of them later.

That makes sense to me, Dana. And, you know what? Even if things started all mixed up, they might still sort out into layers.

How could they do that, Dad?

Let's try another experiment. **(You can try it at home, too.)** Put some water in a peanut butter jar and add a big handful each of gravel, sand, and clay. Then shake it up very well and wait for it to settle. What do you see? **(What do you see at home?)**

Hey! We have three layers! The gravel settled first, then the sand, then the clay. Could fossils settle out that way, too?

Could be. So even if the Flood mixed up some of the ecological zones, we still might get fossils in layers because of the way things settled out in the Flood.

I guess so. But, Dad, wouldn't the Flood sometimes mix up fossils from different groups?

Yes, it would. And sometimes that's what we see — fossil graveyards full of mangled bones from all over the place. For instance, there is a cave in Maryland full of fossil bones. Some of the animals lived in the woods, some on the prairie, some where it's hot, and others where it's cold.

I see. The Flood waters washed them all into the cave area. Do you remember when we went to Agate Springs out in Nebraska, Dad? We saw all those bones jumbled up together. Was that a fossil graveyard, too?

Yes, it was, Dana. So is the group of fossils at Dinosaur National Monument, too, although the mixing isn't as much as in Maryland.

I guess the Flood helps us to explain a lot about fossils.

It surely does, Dana. After all, most fossils start forming when plants and animals get trapped in some kind of flood sediment, like mud or sand.

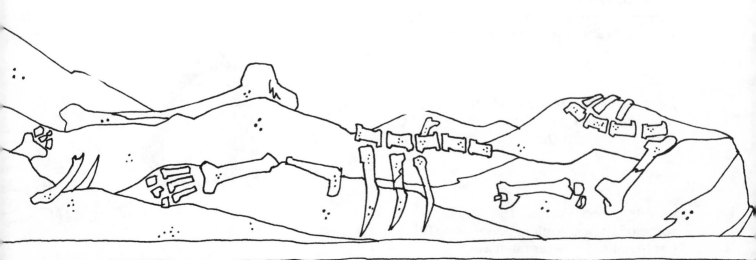

*And the Flood helps us to explain why
certain kinds of plants and animals died out
and became extinct, too.*

Yes. And the Flood also helps us to explain
why fossils come in certain groups, Dana.
That's why we know where to hunt for different kinds of fossils.

*Yes, Dad. Things that lived together got
buried together.*

*I was just thinking, Dad. The fossils help us
to believe the Bible, too.*

Why do you say that?

*Well, what we read in God's Word agrees with
what we see in God's world.*

That's right, Dana! Of course, we believe the
Bible because it is God's Word. But studying
fossils gives us a chance to put that faith
into practice.

Chapter Four

How Old Are Fossils?

The Flood described in the Bible helps scientists to explain many things about fossils. It helps us to explain how fossils were formed, and why they are found all over the world. The Flood also helps us to explain why fossils come in groups, and why so many things have died out or become extinct since Noah's time.

But Noah's Flood happened only a few thousand years ago. And that probably makes you think of another question. My daughter Debbie asked me, too.

Daddy, I have a question. How old are fossils?

Well, Debbie, nobody knows for certain. But, if the fossils are the plants and animals drowned in Noah's Flood, then they would all be about five to seven thousand years old. So that's fairly old, anyway.

Does it take very long for a fossil to form?

Not really. In fact, it has to start very quickly. A plant or animal must be suddenly buried under a heavy load of mud or sand in a flood.

If I buried a snail shell in the back yard, would it turn into a fossil?

Not right away, Debbie. A fossil **starts** when something gets buried. But then you must have the right conditions for it to absorb minerals and change into a fossil.

How long does that take, Daddy?

That depends on the amount of water and kind of rock cement where the plant or animal is buried. It could take only a few years, or maybe a 100 years, or possibly a 1,000 years at the most.

So, I guess there is plenty of time since the Flood to change all the plant and animal remains into fossils. Is that right, Daddy?

Yes, I think so. Do you remember that horse bone Mom found along the creek at Oak Grove back in Iowa?

Oh, yes. One end of it was very hard and rocky just like a fossil. But the other end was sort of soft and squishy like a rotten bone. I guess it didn't take very long for that bone to start becoming a fossil, did it?

Not much time at all! If conditions are not right, a buried plant or animal would never become a fossil. But if conditions are just right, they could turn into a fossil in just a few years.

I just thought of something, Daddy. Fossils were all trapped in Noah's Flood, right? That means they were all alive when Noah was alive. So, that means dinosaurs and trilobites and people all lived at the same time. Is that true?

It surely seems to be, Debbie. The Bible tells us about one man who was with dinosaurs — Job. Job had seen a large land dinosaur called Behemoth, and he knew about a giant reptile called Leviathan that lived in the sea.

Did any other people in history see live dinosaurs?

Yes. There was Alexander the Great, the famous Greek history writer named Herodotus and scientist named Aldrovandus, just to name a few. The scientist had even studied a small dinosaur a farmer had killed.

Debbie, can you imagine what it was like when man and dinosaur lived together?

It is hard to imagine. But if their footprints are found together, I guess dinosaurs and people did live at the same time.

We have evidence that dinosaurs and ocean creatures like trilobites lived at the same time, too.

What evidence is that, Daddy?

Do you know what pollen is, Debbie?

Yes. That's the dusty yellow stuff from flowers that makes you sneeze.

Well, more or less. Anyway, the plants that lived with dinosaurs gave off pollen like plants today. And some of that pollen got trapped and preserved with trilobites.

I see! That means dinosaurs and trilobites did live together.

Almost. Dinosaurs lived in an ecological zone on land, and trilobites lived in the ocean. But some of the pollen from the plants in the dinosaur area blew out into the water and got trapped with the trilobites.

That's what I meant, Daddy! Trilobites and dinosaurs lived at the same time, even if they did live in different places. And if dinosaurs lived with people and with trilobites, then I guess dinosaurs and people and trilobites all lived at the same time. Is that right, Daddy?

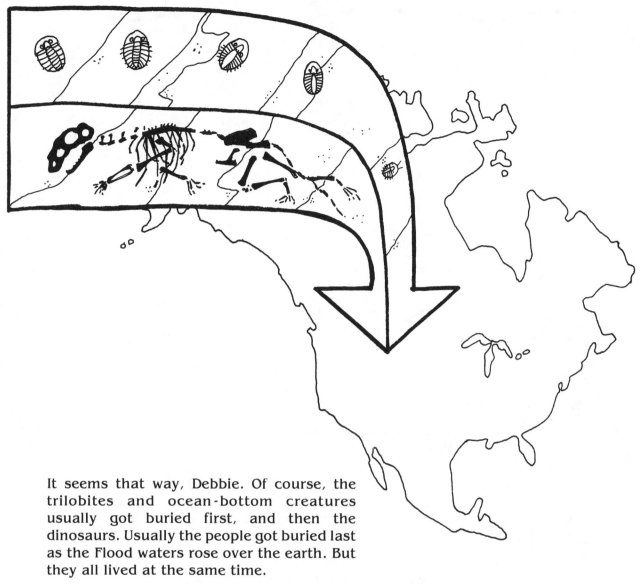

It seems that way, Debbie. Of course, the trilobites and ocean-bottom creatures usually got buried first, and then the dinosaurs. Usually the people got buried last as the Flood waters rose over the earth. But they all lived at the same time.

> *If they all lived at the same time, Daddy, wouldn't the dinosaurs **sometimes** get buried first?*

Yes, and that's just what happened. We are going to a place this summer where rocks from the dinosaurs group are on the bottom and simple ocean creatures are on the top.

> *Where is that, Daddy?*

The Lewis Mountain Range. It starts in Glacier Park in Montana, and runs 350 miles northwest into Canada. The mountain top is a limestone ridge with simple ocean fossils. Underneath is shale rock with shell fossils from the dinosaur group.

> *How did the fossil groups get upside down like that?*

Some people believe the mountain range turned upside down, so to speak.

Mountains turned upside down? How could that happen, Daddy?

Well, Debbie, sometimes earthquakes or volcanoes will cause a small block of rock to split, and then the bottom part is shoved over the top. There are always ground-up rocks and scratch marks to show where the shoving happened.

> *I imagine there are plenty of ground-up rocks and scratches where the ocean fossil rocks were pushed over the dinosaur rocks — especially if the mountain range is 350 miles long!*

You would think so, Debbie. But not where the rock layers touch. The limestone and shale line up smoothly, just like the ocean fossil rock was laid down on top of the dinosaur rock. There doesn't seem to be any shoving at all.

> *Well, if the mountains didn't turn upside down, then why are the fossils upside down?*

It's probably just the way the Flood worked, Debbie. In this area, the Flood washed in some dinosaur zone fossils first. A later current from another direction washed in some simple ocean life. Or maybe the Flood turned the sediment over. Then the "mountains rose up," as the Bible says, at the end of the Flood.

That makes more sense than pretending the mountain turned upside down, Daddy. Besides, it would take something as big as Noah's Flood to shove mountains around anyway!

Right, Debbie. And, of course, you would expect groups to be upside down sometimes. That is, if dinosaurs and trilobites and people all lived at the same time.

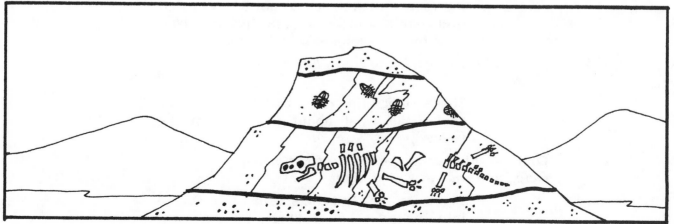

Now you made me think of something else, Daddy. If all these fossil rocks were made in the Flood, then they would be only a few thousand years old, right?

Right, Debbie.

Well, is that enough time to make the Grand Canyon? Wouldn't it take a lot of time to make Grand Canyon?

Either a lot of time, or a lot of water.

What do you mean, Daddy?

Remember when we flew from Chicago to Denver and then to San Diego? When we flew over Iowa you could see the Missouri River. What did it look like?

It was all curled back and forth, like a giant snake.

That's right. The **river** was twisted like a snake. But what about the sides of the valley?

Come to think of it, the sides of the valley were fairly smooth and straight.

Right, Debbie. And the streams that flowed into the river had valleys that narrowed down gradually to a point. But what about Grand Canyon?

Grand Canyon had a very snaky river, but the valleys were all snaky and twisted, too, Daddy.

And the valleys joining the Canyon did not narrow back to a point, either.

Why was there such a big difference, Daddy?

The Missouri River shows what happens when a river cuts its way across fairly flat land. The land around Grand Canyon is flat, too. But Grand Canyon probably started as a crack in the earth during the Flood.

Did earthquakes happen during the Flood, Daddy.

Yes indeed, Debby. Remember, the Bible says that the Flood started when "all the fountains of the great deep burst forth." And at the end of the Flood, "the mountains rose up and the valleys sank down." Grand Canyon seems to be part of a crack in the earth's crust. It starts in Mexico and runs underground all the way up to Yellowstone Park.

Wow! So, Grand Canyon started as sort of an earthquake fault.

Yes, and the Flood waters poured down into the crack from all directions in great abundance. The soft sediments washed away quickly, too, before they turned into rock.

And that would make most of the Canyon form very fast, wouldn't it, Daddy?

That's right, Debbie. And, of course, further erosion has sharpened the features of the Canyon over the past several thousand years since the Flood.

I used to think it would take a long, LONG, time to form fossils and things like the Grand Canyon.

Don't forget, Debbie, that 5,000 years or so since the Flood is quite a long time.

Yes. But many things that look like they would take a long time to form would happen much quicker in the Flood. Right, Daddy?

That's right, Debbie. Another good example is polystratic (**polly 'străt ick**) fossils.

Polly-what fossils?

Polystratic fossils. They are fossils that cut through many rock layers.

What is so important about those kinds of fossils, Daddy?

Well, sometimes a tree trunk or a big shellfish cuts across many layers of rock.

What does that mean?

Now, think a minute, Debbie. Suppose it took a long time to form one rock layer, then a long time for the next and the next. What would happen to the tree trunk or shell?

I guess the top would rot away or break off.

Exactly. But in these polystratic fossils, the top isn't rotten and the shell isn't broken.

Oh, now I understand. That means all the rock layers and fossils had to be buried in a hurry. Otherwise, the tree or shell would rot and break off.

That's right, Debbie. And there are many fossils like that in coal, too.

Daddy, that reminds me. Doesn't it take a long time to form coal and oil?

Not really, Debbie. They can be formed in a science laboratory in just a few hours. So a few thousand years since the Flood should be plenty of time.

What about those long, pointed things in caves, Daddy? Do you remember the ones we saw in Carlsbad Caverns in New Mexico and at those caves in Kentucky?

You mean stalactites **(sta 'lack tites)** and stalagmites **(sta 'lag mites)**, Debbie?

Yes, that's it. Don't they take a long time to form?

Not if conditions are right, and if you have a lot of mineral water. In one cave they grew so fast that they covered a dead bat before it had time to decay!

And that's what the fossils tell us, too. We just find different varieties of the plants and animals God created, like we have today. And they lived in ecological zones much like we have today, too.

Yes, except for extinction. Because of sin, the world was corrupted, and God destroyed that first sinful world with the Flood.

And that's what the fossils tell us, too. The fossils are all the plants and animals that were drowned and buried in the Flood.

That's right, Debbie. But that's not the end of the story. What does the Bible tell us about the future?

That Jesus Christ will come again and make all things new.

Amen, Debbie. "Even so, come quickly, Lord Jesus."

Okay, Daddy. But I still have one more question. Why is it that everybody is always saying that fossils are millions of years old?

There are many different reasons, Debbie. For one thing, if you didn't believe in God, you would probably have to believe fossils are very old.

Why is that?

Well, if you didn't believe God created life, then you would have to believe that life made itself by chance. It takes a long time to make something by chance. Imagine how much longer it would take to shake together a jig-saw puzzle by chance than to put one together on purpose!

But if God created things like He says in the Bible, that wouldn't take so long, would it, Daddy?

No, it wouldn't, Debbie. The Bible tells us that God created all the different kinds of life in a short time. And He made them to live and multiply together in harmony.

Chapter Five

Fossils — Evolution or Creation?

My family and I surely enjoyed taking your imagination on some fossil hunting trips with us. (Maybe we'll even see you at the Museum in San Diego sometime, or out on the fossil hunting trail!)

I also hope you have seen that the things we know about fossils agree with what we read in God's Word, the Bible.

But you have probably heard about another view, too. It's called "evolution" **(ev ō 'lū shun)**. My son, David, was asking me about that.

Dad, we have been talking a lot about fossils and Creation and the Flood.

Sounds like you have a question, Dave.

Well, I was telling a friend at school about fossils. He said that we are all wrong. He said that fossils prove evolution.

A lot of people believe that.

What is evolution, anyway?

Well, David, today evolution is the idea that life started billions of years ago by chance. Then, according to evolution, living things gradually changed and became more complex. Evolution is supposed to go from fish to frog to lizard, and then to birds and hairy animals, and finally to man.

That's quite a story! So evolution tells how some fishes changed to lizards and how some lizards changed to people.

That's the idea.

If that's the evolution idea, Dad, what is the creation idea?

According to the creation idea, David, God created many different kinds of life that were complex right from the beginning. Then because of our sin, God sent the Flood. Many living things were buried and turned into fossils. Some became extinct.

That's quite a different idea! Do the fossils prove evolution or creation?

They don't **prove** either idea, but they really give the best support to creation.

*That's what **you** say, Dad. The people who believe in evolution probably think the fossils support their idea.*

Not all of them. Many famous evolution scientists believe the fossils hurt evolution and help creation. Did you ever hear of Charles Darwin?

I think so. Isn't he the man that thought up the idea of evolution?

Yes, he is. Do you know what Darwin thought about fossils, David?

I guess he thought fossils were proof for evolution.

No. Just the opposite. Darwin said that fossils were "perhaps the most obvious and serious objection" to his theory.

Really, Dad? Why did he say that?

Because he knew the same things about fossils that we know, Dave.

What's that?

Well, you have found many fossil snails and clams and trilobites. Did you ever find a "snam" or a "clamobite," or something in between a snail and a clam, or between a clam and a trilobite?

No, Dad. Don't be silly.

I'm not, Dave. If evolution were true, then there should be fossils to show how one kind of life changed into another.

Yes. Oh, I understand now. All we find are clams and snails and things, with no in-between forms. So, I guess that would be evidence for creation. Right, Dad?

That's right, David.

62

What do people who believe in evolution say about in-between forms?

Well, David, evolutionists know that you don't find the in-between forms. They call them **"missing links."** Some scientists are still looking for missing links. But many scientists nowadays say that nobody will ever find missing links for evolution. After all, snails, clams, jellyfish, and complex squids are the "first" or "deepest" fossils we find.

What about plants? Did anyone ever find missing links for plants?

No. Darwin knew that, too. He called the origin of plants a "mystery."

Now I remember. The seed plants we find as fossils are just oaks, willows, pines, palms, and plants like we have today.

That's right, David. Dr. Corner, a famous evolutionary biologist at Cambridge University, once said, ". . . to the unprejudiced, the fossil record of plants is in favor of special creation."

*Don't people who believe in evolution have
any evidence for their side, Dad?*

Maybe, Dave. There is one very odd fossil
that appears somewhat halfway between a
lizard and a bird.

It does? What is it called?

Archaeopteryx **(Ark ē 'ŏp ter iks).**

Archie . . . Archie . . . what?

Let's just call it the "Archie-bird," Dave.

*That's okay with me, Dad! Does that Archie-
bird really appear to be halfway between a
lizard and a bird?*

In a way it does. It has feathers and a beak
like a bird. But it has teeth in its beak and a
long, bony tail somewhat like a lizard.

*I guess that does prove evolution after all,
doesn't it?*

Wait a minute, David! What about all the
evidence for creation in clams and snails
and plants and man and other kinds of
fossils? It's not just one fossil, it's the whole
weight of evidence that favors creation!

Oh, yes. But what about that in-between lizard-bird?

First of all, it's not so in-between as you might think. Some extinct birds had teeth, and some lizards don't have teeth, so that's not so important.

I see. But what about the feathers?

Evolutionists believe that scales changed into feathers. But the "Archie-bird" has many different kinds of feathers. These feathers are all completely developed, just as those of birds living today.

That's more like evidence for creation instead of evolution, isn't it, Dad?

It surely is. And there's one more thing, too, David.

What's that?

Recently, scientists found fossils of just ordinary birds as deep in the fossil rocks as the "Archie-bird."

Wow! I guess "Archie-birds" couldn't change into birds if birds were already here!

You're right about that, Dave. As far as what the fossils show, snails have always been snails, and birds have always been birds, right from the beginning.

That brings up another question, Dad. You were telling me that the fossils were probably things drowned in the Flood. Right?

Yes, Dave.

And so, the fossils were alive at Noah's time and are probably only a few thousand years old. Right?

Right.

Well, my friend who told me about evolution showed me a book. It said that fossils are millions of years old. He said you could prove it with uranium (ū 'raın ē ŭm) dating.

If you use uranium to date fossil rocks, **sometimes** you do get ages in millions of years. **But,** did your friend also tell you about scientists at Oak Ridge National Laboratories?

No. What about them, Dad?

They used uranium dating on wood in rocks of the dinosaur group and got ages of only thousands of years.

Really?

Yes, David. And besides that, scientists got dates of 169 million and 3 billion years for two Hawaiian lava flows. But these lava flows happened less than 200 years ago, in 1800 and 1801!

66

I guess uranium isn't proof after all, is it.

> I don't think it is. But don't just take my word for it, David. You read what the Bible says, and study the science for yourself when you get older. I want you to know what you think for your own good reasons.

You know, Dad, I was just thinking. If there isn't really any proof of evolution, why do people believe it?

> Not because of the fossils, that's for sure. The fossils go along with creation. But I can tell you why I once believed in evolution.

YOU believed in EVOLUTION?

> Yes, I did, David. I even taught it in college for several years.

Really?? Why did you believe in evolution, Dad?

> I **thought** I believed it because of all the evidence. I **really** believed it because I didn't believe in God.

You *didn't believe in God, Dad?*

> Not really, Dave. I surely didn't believe that God was speaking to me through the Bible. And, after all, there is **one big weak** spot in the creation view.

What is that?

> You can't believe in creation if you don't believe in a Creator. If there is no Creator, then creation doesn't make any sense.

But if there is a Creator, then evolution doesn't make any sense.

> You are right about that for sure, David! Evolution is **not** based on the fossil evidence. It is really based on belief that you have to explain everything without God.

So, creation and evolution are both really a matter of faith.

> When you get to the bottom of it, that's true, Dave. If you don't believe in God, then you have to believe in some kind of evolution. And then you must try to make the fossils fit in with evolution somehow.

But if you believe the Bible, then you can see how easily the fossils fit with Creation, man's sin, and the Flood. Right, Dad?

> Right, Dave!

Just wait until I tell my friend that the fossils
go along with creation instead of evolution!

Hold it! Wait a minute, Dave. Do you think that you can make your friend quit believing evolution and start believing creation just because the fossil evidence supports creation?

Sure. Why not?

Remember in John 6 where Jesus was preaching right after He fed the 5,000 men? The people became angry and asked Him to do a miracle.

I remember. What does that mean, Dad?

It means that the people had just watched Jesus do all kinds of miracles. He even raised people from the dead. But just like Jesus said, "If they won't believe Moses and the prophets, they won't believe, even if someone rises from the dead."

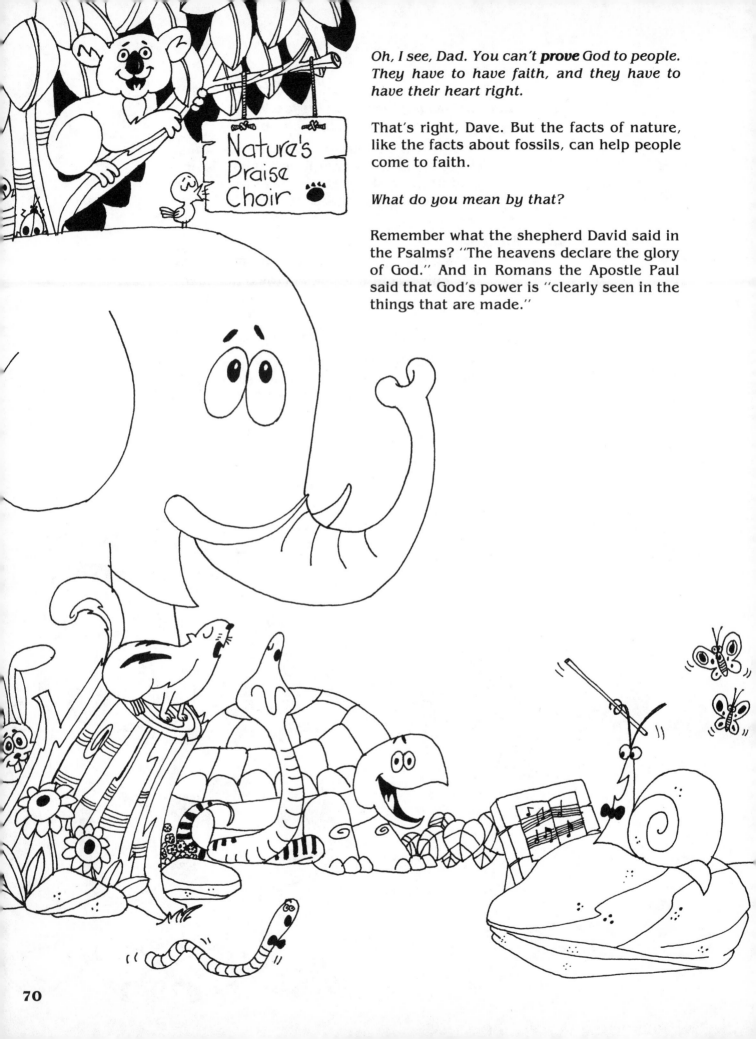

*Oh, I see, Dad. You can't **prove** God to people. They have to have faith, and they have to have their heart right.*

That's right, Dave. But the facts of nature, like the facts about fossils, can help people come to faith.

What do you mean by that?

Remember what the shepherd David said in the Psalms? "The heavens declare the glory of God." And in Romans the Apostle Paul said that God's power is "clearly seen in the things that are made."

So, I can tell my friend all about fossils, and maybe God will use it to help change his heart. Is that the idea?

It surely is, Dave. But go easy. Remember your own Dad believed in evolution for years and years. Like Peter says, "be able to give a reason for the hope that is within you, but in **meekness** and **gentleness.**"

Okay, Dad, I'll try.

And we hope that you, too, will try to see God's world through God's eyes. The heavens declare His glory; the fossils show the power of His judgment. And the open arms of Jesus hold us with the love of God that leads to abundant life forever for those who believe Him.

Thanks for sharing our adventures and thoughts on fossils. From our family to you and yours — May God bless you!

71

Dr. Gary Parker's New Book . . .

LIFE BEFORE BIRTH

A Christian Family Book

Also with Read-along Cassette

Life is special. In the style of *Dry Bones and Other Fossils*, Dr. Parker and his wife, Mary, explain the Biblical concepts of life before birth to their ''children.'' The topics of abortion and birth defects are covered in a special way — important to developing a Christ-centered world view.